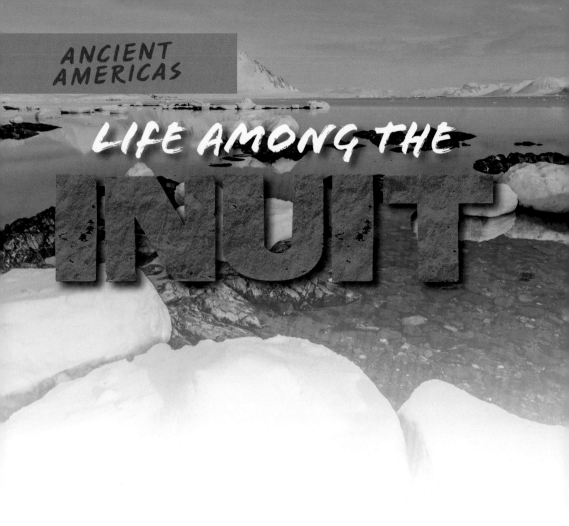

ANCIENT
AMERICAS

LIFE AMONG THE
INUIT

IAN MAHANEY

PowerKiDS
press™

NEW YORK

Published in 2017 by **The Rosen Publishing Group**
29 East 21st Street, New York, NY 10010

Developed and produced for Rosen by BlueAppleWorks Inc.

Art Director: Haley Harasymiw
Managing Editor for BlueAppleWorks: Melissa McClellan
Editor: Marcia Abramson
Design: T.J. Choleva

Picture credits: Cover: frgrd. Ansgar Walk/Wikimedia; bkgrd. Daderot/Wikimedia. Back cover: frgrd. Artishok/
Shutterstock; bkgrd. altanaka/Shutterstock. Title page, p 9 Incredible Arctic/Shutterstock; p. 5 U.S. National
Archives and Records Administration/Public Domain; p. 5 Edward S. Curtis/Wikimedia; p. 6 Royal Canadian
Mounted Police/Library and Archives Canada/C-089343; p. 6 right Jagodka/Shutterstock; p. 7 Edward Henry,
Harriman/Public Domain; p. 10Nadezhda Bolotina/Shutterstock; p. 10 right jackf/Shutterstock; p. 14 inset
National Museum of Canada/Library and Archives Canada/e004665163; p. 14 Frank E. Kleinschmidt/Library
of Congress/Public Domain; p. 15 top, 19, 21 Public Domain; p. 15 bottom Daderot/Creative Commons; p.
16 jai MANSSON/Creative Commons; p. 16 inset Lisa Risager/Creative Commons; p. 17 Library of Congress/
Public Domain; p. 18 top left Sophia Granchinho/Shutterstock; p. 19 left Kiugak Ashoona/Creative Commons;
p. 22 Nasjonalbiblioteket/Creative Commons; p. 23 Edward S. Curtis/Public Domain; p. 24 James Laurence
Cotter/Public Domain; p. 25 inset Robert J. Flaherty/Public Domain; p. 25 Th. N. Krabbe/Creative Commons;
p. 25 right Didier Descouens/Creative Commons; p. 27, 29 Ansgar Walk/Creative Commons; p. 28 furtseff/
Shutterstock; Maps: p 11 T.J. Choleva /Intrepix/Shutterstock

Cataloging-in-Publication Data

Names: Mahaney, Ian.
Title: Life among the Inuit / Ian Mahaney.
Description: New York : PowerKids Press, 2017. | Series: Ancient Americas | Includes index.
Identifiers: ISBN 9781508149873 (pbk.) | ISBN 9781508149811 (library bound) | ISBN 9781508149699 (6 pack)
Subjects: LCSH: Inuit--Juvenile literature.
Classification: LCC E99.E7 M34 2017| DDC 973'.04971--dc23

Manufactured in the United States of America

CPSIA Compliance Information: Batch #BS16PK: For Further Information contact Rosen Publishing, New York, New York at 1-800-237-9932

CONTENTS

CHAPTER 1

PEOPLE OF THE NORTH

The last ice age began between 120,000 and 60,000 years in the past. It peaked about 20,000 years ago and lasted for another 10,000 years. During this ice age, sea levels fell, exposing the seafloor of the Bering Strait. Today the Bering Strait is a small body of water that connects the Arctic Ocean to the Pacific Ocean. Russia is west of the strait and Alaska is east. At its narrowest point, the Bering Strait is less than 55 miles (89 km) wide.

Archaeologists and **anthropologists** think many **nomadic** people crossed the land bridge from Siberia, now a part of Russia, to Alaska. The Siberians likely followed herds of animals east into Alaska. They moved east as they sought better hunting. They survived by hunting animals for food and clothing along the way.

Some of these migrants moved south into areas that are modern-day Canada and the continental United States. Other peoples stayed north. Researchers believe the Siberians crossed in several waves. The first arrivals spread out, while some later migrants stayed in Alaska. Some Siberians even made homes on the land bridge, but when the ice started melting and the sea rose, they also migrated.

THE INUIT PEOPLES OF THE ARCTIC SHARE COMMON ANCESTORS, LANGUAGE, AND CULTURES.

5

The travelers who stayed in northern Alaska became ancestors of Yupik and Aleut people that still live there. The Inuit descended from a different group that began spreading out from Alaska about A.D. 1000, reaching across Canada all the way to Greenland. Anthropologists call this group the Thule culture after a town in Greenland. They hunted, fished, and adapted to the frigid environment.

The Siberians had brought their dogs with them across the land bridge, and dogs played a key role in helping them to adapt. Dogs carried packs and pulled sleds on land and ice. They helped with hunting and barked warnings when strangers and dangerous animals came near. Today's huskies and Malamutes continue to be working dogs as well as pets. In fact, the Arctic territory of Nunavut has adopted the Canadian Inuit dog as its official symbol.

INUITS HAVE BEEN BREEDING HUSKIES FOR THOUSANDS OF YEARS.

The Inuit lifestyle has changed in the past 500 years since the Inuit met European explorers. These explorers traveled to Canada and the Hudson Bay in northeastern Canada. Some searched for a shortcut from the Atlantic Ocean to the Pacific Ocean that passed through North America. Other Europeans arrived on whaling ships.

When the Inuit met Europeans, many caught European diseases they had never been exposed to before such as measles and influenza. Large populations of Inuit died from these diseases. In some ways, the Inuit benefited, too. Europeans introduced the Inuit to metal that they used for harpoon tips. Rifles made hunting easier, and they began hunting more so they could trade furs. Because of this fur trade, the Inuit turned less nomadic. They needed a stable location to trade. Their lives began to change.

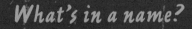

What's in a name?

For a long time, the Arctic peoples were usually called Eskimos. The word's origin is unclear, but many Inuit dislike it. "Inuit," which means "the people," is widely used today, especially in Canada and Greenland.

7

CHAPTER 2

HARSH INUIT WORLD

The Inuit and all other peoples who live or have lived in the Arctic inhabit an area with a harsh climate. Depending on where someone lives, the sun may not rise for months during the winter. At the North Pole, the sun never rises from October to March. Further south within the Arctic Circle where the Inuit live, darkness lasts a shorter period of time. On many consecutive days, though, the sun never rises. It is thus very cold. The coldest temperature ever recorded in the United States was recorded in Alaska in 1971. It was -80° Fahrenheit (-62° C).

During summer months, the sun is in the sky all day in the Arctic. It is still chilly, though. During the summer, the average temperature at the North Pole is 40 degrees Fahrenheit (4° C). Though the sun shines all day, the sun remains low on the **horizon**. Few plants and trees grow in the Arctic. Strong winds dominate the landscape.

The Inuit adapted to harsh winters and cool summers. They modified their lives around the supplies they could find or hunt. They hunted for meat and made warm coats from the skins and furs of animals they killed. The Inuit burned the oil of seals they hunted. During summers they built shelters supported by whale bones.

THE NORTHERN LIGHTS, OR **AURORA BOREALIS**, OFTEN GLOW IN THE ARCTIC SKY AND FARTHER SOUTH. INUIT LEGENDS SAY THE LIGHTS ARE SPIRITS DANCING.

The Inuit adapted to the cold by building igloos made of ice to keep warm through the winter months. They traveled the land by dogsled. To make it easier to walk on snow and ice, Inuit strapped snowshoes to their boots. Snowshoes are platforms made of wood and leather strips that help spread the wearer's weight on a larger area and can balance on top of the snow rather than sinking into it. Walking on snow was not the only problem. With snow covering everything, it could be difficult to see, causing a condition called snow blindness. So the Inuit invented snow goggles. They carved the goggles out of antlers, bone, or wood, with a narrow slit for looking out. They tied their goggles on with a thin strip of caribou **sinew**.

THE CARIBOU IS WELL ADAPTED TO COLD CLIMATES. IT GROWS HOLLOW-HAIRED FUR THAT PROVIDES INSULATION FROM HARSH WINTER WEATHER.

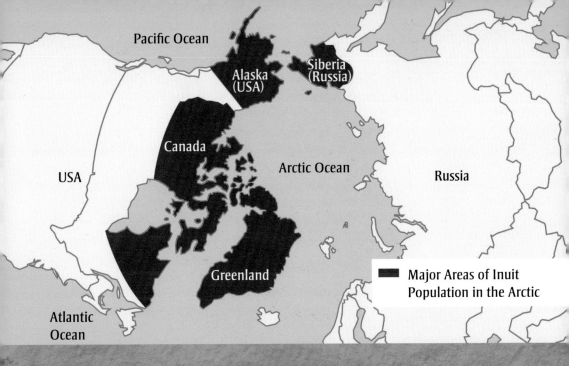

Pacific Ocean

Alaska (USA)

Siberia (Russia)

Canada

Arctic Ocean

Russia

USA

Greenland

Atlantic Ocean

■ Major Areas of Inuit Population in the Arctic

INUIT GROUPS

There were similarities and differences among the Inuit living in its three major regions in northern Alaska, northern Canada, and Greenland. In common, the Inuit coped with a harsh landscape. They hunted. They fished. They also have a common language, Inuktitut. Though they speak different **dialects** in northern Alaska, northern Canada, Greenland, and Russia, the Inuit still understand one another. Some Inuit remained by the coast and hunted mainly sea mammals such as seals, walruses, and whales. Other Inuit groups, especially those of the central Inuit who lived in northern Canada, moved frequently to follow herds of caribou. The caribou lived in the **tundra** during summer when they ate the vegetation. There was no vegetation in the winter so the herds moved south to forests. The central Inuit followed the caribou while coastal Inuit remained closer to the shore year-round.

CHAPTER 3

LIFE AMONG INUITS

Men did the hunting and fishing in traditional Inuit families, while women cooked, sewed, and cared for children. Women were not barred from hunting, though, and some did. Men learned to sew and cook, too. The contributions of both sexes were valued by the community.

Inuit families of a mother, father, and children helped each other. The men often hunted together when they targeted large mammals such as whales and walruses. The women stayed with the children. Women cooked and made clothing for their families. Women's skills at sewing were very important as the family spent many days outside. These women taught their daughters to cook and sew. Boys stayed home until they were ready to join their fathers and hunt.

Getting married

Marriages were arranged by Inuit families. Girls often married in their early teens but boys had to grow into good hunters before starting a family.

IN ORDER TO SURVIVE IN SUCH A COLD LAND, INUITS DEVELOPED STRONG COMMUNITIES WHERE EVERYONE HELPED EACH OTHER.

13

INUIT DWELLINGS

Men also built houses. Most Inuit were nomadic, following the herds of animals they hunted. During the long winter, they quickly put together houses out of ice and snow. An igloo could be built in just a few hours! They cut blocks of ice from the ground's surface and built walls and a dome from the blocks. They filled in cracks with snow and more ice. The families insulated the walls with skins, and burned whale or seal oil for heat and light. Igloos kept families surprisingly warm. When summer arrived, the camps broke up into smaller hunting groups, often no larger than a single family. During the summer hunts, the families lived in tents made of sealskin or caribou hides.

"IGLOO" HAS COME TO MEAN A SNOW HOUSE, BUT THE ORIGINAL INUIT WORD DESCRIBED ANY KIND OF HOUSE.

INUITS MADE CLOTHING BY HAND FROM SKINS AND FURS. EACH PIECE WAS SNUG AT THE OPENINGS TO KEEP THE COLD OUT.

INUIT CLOTHING

To keep warm, Inuits traditionally wore layers of clothing with fur-lined hoods, mittens, and boots. Animal skins had to be cleaned and softened before they could be sewn, and even then, sewing was hard work. Women used ivory or bone needles, with animal sinews for thread. Men and women wore anoraks, which are like long parkas, with one or two pairs of pants underneath. One anorak was worn fur side in, with a second over it, fur side out. For babies, mothers would sew a carrying pouch into their anorak, and make jumpsuits out of fur for little ones to wear.

15

FOOD GATHERING AND PREPARATION

Inuit women spent much time cooking and preparing food. They fed their families the animals their husbands hunted. Depending on the season and their location, they hunted for animals such as fish, seals, walrus, and caribou. Inuits also ate birds and their eggs.

The Inuit often dried fish they caught during the summer to eat in winter. Both men and women fished. They hung strips of fish such as arctic char and lit a fire beneath the fish until the fire dried and preserved the fish. During the summer, families gathered berries.

Hunters often started eating meat raw as soon as they killed it. Then they brought the carcass home, and the women cooked the rest of the meat for everyone to share.

MUKTUK IS EATEN RAW, COOKED, OR PICKLED. IT IS MADE OF FROZEN WHALE SKIN AND BLUBBER.

A favorite **delicacy** was called kiviaq. The Inuit stuffed seabirds into a seal skin and let the birds ferment in their pouch for months.

In winter, the Inuit would eat caribou, moose, crab, whale, seal, various fish, walrus, ducks, geese, and sometimes seaweed. In summer they added roots and berries, but even so, their traditional diet was high in protein and fat. Scientists wondered why they did not get sick from lack of fruits and vegetables. Then they discovered that the Inuit got the missing vitamins and nutrients from eating all the parts of animals, even organs that most people would discard. Adequate vitamin C could be obtained from items in their traditional diet of raw meat such as ringed seal liver and whale skin (muktuk).

STONE MARKERS - THE INUKSHUKS

The Inuit built stone sculptures called "inukshuks" across the Arctic. The name means "likeness of human." The sculptures helped the Inuit survive by marking good fishing or hunting spots. Some served as **navigational** aids, pointing out the right path with humanlike arms. Others were built as memorials. The inukshuks became a powerful symbol of the Inuit. The **emblem** for the 2010 Winter Olympics held in Canada was based on the inukshuk.

INUIT RELIGION AND WORSHIP

The Inuit held the animals they hunted in high regard. The people believed that every living creature had a soul. If they respected the animals and their souls then the Inuit would continue to successfully hunt for years to come.

The Inuit also believed in a spiritual world. Most collections of Inuit families had a **shaman** who communicated with this spiritual world. For example, the shaman communicated with Sedna, the goddess of the sea. The Inuit passed several myths of Sedna's origin from generation to generation. In one origin myth, Sedna follows a bird home. Sedna is unhappy with the bird's housing and food supplies so Sedna asks her father to come for her. In their escape, Sedna's father kills the bird, but other birds try to punish Sedna. To escape, the father pushes Sedna into the ocean where her fingers turn into seals and other animals. She becomes the goddess of the sea. The Inuit found stories and myths like Sedna important. Elder Inuit people explained the world to children through stories.

TOOLS AND ART

The Inuit, who never wasted anything, made their tools, weapons, and utensils from natural materials, such as ivory, stone, and animal skins and bones. For example, a bow drill was made with rib bones from caribou or whales and sealskin rope.

The Inuit used the same natural materials to create artwork, an important part of their culture since the beginning. The first Siberian migrants left behind a few ivory carvings that have been discovered by archaeologists. As the culture developed, the Inuit carved small sculptures out of ivory, bone, and soft stone to depict animals and people. Storytellers used these, along with masks and **amulets**, to act out myths and history. People all over the world now enjoy and collect Inuit art.

EVEN USING AN INUIT BOW DRILL, IT WAS NOT EASY TO DRILL THROUGH BONE TO MAKE OTHER TOOLS.

CHAPTER 4

HUNTING PROWESS OF INUITS

The Inuit survived in the harsh Arctic because they utilized the animals there so well. There was no way to farm, so they caught fish, birds, and small and large mammals on land, ice, and sea. Every part of the animal was turned into something useful.

The hunters banded together to hunt large mammals such as whales and walruses. They also hunted polar bears. The hunters remained on land to search for smaller but no less dangerous mammals such as wolves. In addition to hunting and fishing with hooks, spears, and harpoons, the Inuit used bows and arrows to hunt caribou. They chased polar bears on dogsleds and attacked with spears. They hunted with the best tools for their target.

FISHING WITH SPEARS AND HOOKS

Inuit fishermen caught fish using different methods depending on the season. In winter, they cut holes in the ice and caught fish using a fish lure and spear. During the summer, fishermen built stone traps in rivers. When fish swam into the trap, the Inuit fishermen used spears to capture and kill the fish. These spears were called kakivaks. The Inuit ate many types of fish including Arctic char, cod, and trout.

LIKE FISHERMEN ALL OVER THE WORLD, INUIT USED A LURE ON A LINE TO ATTRACT FISH. INSTEAD OF REELING FISH IN, THOUGH, THE INUIT WOULD SPEAR THEM.

21

SEALING A DEAL

Seals have always been special animals for the Inuit. They provided meat, fat to make lamp oil, and waterproof skin for clothing, tents, and boots. According to legend, the first Inuit and the seals made an agreement that the Inuit would hunt seals only to feed their families. If they became greedy, they would anger the seals. The seals would stop reproducing and disappear.

To show their respect for the seals and the agreement, Inuit hunters always offered a drink of fresh water to a dying seal. This courtesy also pleased the sea goddess Sedna so that she would keep plenty of food in her sea.

SEAL HUNTING

The Inuit hunted all kinds of seals, but especially the plentiful ringed seal, their main food source in winter months. Harp seals and bearded seals also were hunted. Depending on the season, they used different hunting methods.

In winter, hunters and their dogs found holes in the sea ice. Seals scratched and poked holes in the ice so they could surface to breathe. The hunters waited near the hole for their prey to come up. Polar bears used the same hunting technique, so perhaps the Inuit learned it from them! Once a seal surfaced for air, the Inuit hunter attacked his target with a spear.

HUNTING IN KAYAKS

The Inuit also hunted seals during the summer on the open sea. They rode in long, narrow kayaks, made from driftwood and covered with sealskins. The Inuit had an easy time navigating water in these boats because of their design. Kayaks rarely tip over and even if they do, the kayaker can roll the boat over to float again.

The Inuit used kayaks for transportation as well, but they were important vehicles for seal hunting. On the open water, the hunter kept a spear or harpoon made of driftwood with a bone or stone tip in the boat. He attacked the seal when the animal surfaced. Each hunter had a custom-made kayak for his size and weight.

THE NAME MEANS "HUNTER'S BOAT," BUT KAYAKS ARE NOW POPULAR FOR RECREATION ALL OVER THE WORLD.

BELUGA WHALES, ALSO KNOWN AS WHITE WHALES, OFTEN WERE HUNTED AS JUVENILES, WHEN THEY ARE EASIER TO KILL AND TASTIER TO EAT.

WHALE HUNTING

In areas where whales were abundant, whale hunting provided a plentiful supply of food. The Inuit mainly hunted beluga and bowhead whales. The smaller belugas were easier to catch, but a giant bowhead could feed a village for a whole year with its meat, skin, and blubber. A bowhead can grow to 50 feet (15 m) long and weigh 60 tons (54,431 kg). Its mouth alone can be about 16 feet (4.9 m) long and 8 feet (2.4 m) wide.

Many hunters were needed to make the difficult attack on a whale. When hunting whales, the Inuit rode in umiaks. Umiaks were large boats made of driftwood and walrus or sealskin that could hold many hunters.

About twenty hunters rode in each umiak. Others came along in kayaks. They carried harpoons with a sharp metal tip that could be detached. The hunters could pull back the shaft of the harpoon, put on a new point, and strike again.

The hunters also attached balloons made from sealskin to harpoons. The air-filled balloons kept the whale from swimming fast or diving deep to escape. Even so, it could take a long time to tire out and catch a single whale.

UMIAKS COULD BE PADDLED OR ROWED WITH OARS. THEY OFTEN WERE USED TO CARRY FAMILIES OR CARGO.

CHAPTER 5

PRESENT ERA AND LEGACY

About 800 years ago, the Inuit met their first Europeans. The Vikings sailed to Greenland from Iceland in about A.D. 1200 and later reached the shores of North America. Inuit groups did not have much if any contact with Europeans again until the sixteenth century when they met European fur traders and explorers. The explorers searched for the Northwest Passage. The Northwest Passage is a **theoretical** trading route that connects the Atlantic and Pacific oceans. It is theoretical because the route is full of sea ice and difficult to navigate. The explorers were looking for a route through Inuit land. It's not surprising the Inuit met Europeans.

During the 1800s, more Europeans arrived in Inuit lands to trade. The Inuit groups traded furs from animals they had hunted for food, guns, and other **provisions**. Other Europeans came to Inuit lands as **missionaries**.

The Inuit lifestyle began to change after this contact with Europeans. Inuit lands were eventually absorbed by different countries. The new rulers made the Inuit follow new laws. The Inuit are no longer a nomadic people following animals for their food.

INUITS TODAY MAY WEAR TRADITIONAL CLOTHES, STORE-BOUGHT GARMENTS, OR A COMBINATION.

27

GLOBAL WARMING

Although the Inuit have adapted well to their frigid environment, they are being forced to change again in the twenty-first century. Global warming, which is a gradual increase in the temperature of the Earth, has upset the lives of the Inuit and the animals they depend on. Much sea ice has melted and continues to melt. Igloos melt faster, too. There is less snow and ice available to make igloos, so other types of shelter must be built. In addition, the changes in the icy landscape are making it difficult for hunters to navigate on their usual routes. Hunting seasons are different as well, and scientists think that caribou and polar bear, two important animals for the Inuit, are becoming endangered species. Some Inuit fear their way of life is disappearing.

About 160,000 Inuit live in the Arctic today, with more than 50,000 each in Canada and Greenland, plus smaller groups in Alaska and Russia. These Inuit are citizens of those countries, too. They follow the laws and have changed their lives. They rarely drive dogsleds today, but the Inuit ride snowmobiles and drive cars instead.

Many Inuit live in settlements like villages today. They live in wooden houses and enjoy modern conveniences. They still live in a land where it is dark for most of the winter, but they have electricity and furnaces in their houses. They play video games, have televisions, and even access the Internet. They go to school.

Depending on in which country they live they learn English, Dutch, or Russian, but study Inuit traditions and languages, too.

The Inuit people have a strong culture. Many Inuit, while not resistant to change, are trying to hold onto their culture. They want to pass the culture to new generations while embracing modern conveniences.

Hunting remains an important part of that culture, even as the environment and the animal life change in the Inuits' Arctic homeland. Although they can buy food at grocery stores, many Inuit people still make fish and game the **staple** of their diet. Families fish and hunt together, not only for food, but to share their heritage and enjoy the natural world around them.

GUNS AND SNOWMOBILES HAVE MOSTLY REPLACED SPEARS AND DOGSLEDS FOR HUNTING.

GLOSSARY

amulet: a small charm worn to protect against evil or bad luck

anthropologists: scientists who study the history and society of humans

archaeologists: scientists who study the remains of peoples from the past to understand how they lived

aurora borealis: bands of light that have a magnetic and electrical source and appear at night in the Arctic

blubber: the fat on whales and some other aquatic animals

delicacy: something pleasing to eat that is uncommon

dialects: different ways that a language is spoken in different areas

emblem: a design or figure used as an identifying mark

horizon: a line where the sky seems to meet the earth

missionaries: people who go to a foreign country to do religious work

navigational: relating to steering a boat or other vehicle

nomadic: roaming about from place to place

provisions: food and supplies

shaman: a person who is believed to communicate with a spiritual world

sinew: a cord or band of tissue connecting a muscle with bone

staple: an item, often food, that is used and needed regularly

theoretical: possibly true but not yet proven

tundra: a cold, treeless area with permanently frozen soil

FOR MORE INFORMATION

BOOKS

Cunningham, Kevin, and Peter Benoit. *The Inuit*. New York: Children's Press, 2011.

Lynch, Wayne. *Planet Arctic: Life at the Top of the World*. Richmond Hill, CN: Firefly Books, 2012.

Spillsbury, Louise. *Igloos and Inuit Life*. North Mankato, MN: Capstone, 2011.

Stern, Pamela R. *Daily Life of the Inuit*. Santa Barbara, CA. ABC-CLIO, 2010.

WEBSITES

Because of the changing nature of Internet links, PowerKids Press has developed an online list of websites related to the subject of this book. This site is updated regularly. Please use this link to access the list:

www.powerkidslinks.com/aa/inuit

INDEX

32

11/14